Monster Monologues

Patricia Nelson

Fernwood
PRESS

Monster Monologues

©2025 by Patricia Nelson

Fernwood Press
Newberg, Oregon
www.fernwoodpress.com

All rights reserved. No part may be reproduced
for any commercial purpose by any method without
permission in writing from the copyright holder.

Printed in the United States of America

Cover and page design: Eric Muhr
Cover photo is of 1973P44 Circe, an 1893 bronze sculpture by Sir Edgar Bertram
 Mackennal, held by Birmingham Museums
Author photo: John Andrew Murphy

ISBN 978-1-59498-175-3

The monsters that most of us knew only through the language of the myths had little to do with us, the human beings who read them. Some of us devoured them, even though we knew them only as timeworn interpretations. Patricia Nelson, however, has taken these myths we thought we knew well and revealed them in their ambiguous ways, their truly human versions of ourselves. We see the ancient monsters not as fabulations of Otherness but as metaphors for how we, as humans, navigate our lives.

As always with Patricia's poems, we are invited to view our own lives through a deep recasting of the original stories, totally new retellings. Her language and mastery of poetry filled with original uses of insightful metaphor and poetic imagery raise our understanding of the monsters of myth to a new level. *Monster Monologues* is an important book both for its poetry and its conceptual basis of the world of myth.

—Fran Claggett-Holland
author of *The Shape a Wing Makes*
and *Under the Wings of the Crow*

From the serpentine monster with the "thumb-wide, hissing spine" to her concluding thirsty land animal, Patricia Nelson brings us a collection of poems featuring dragons, Shakespearean villains, Greek mythological figures, and other assorted characters. She carefully interrogates what lies beneath the surfaces of life. Her carefully composed, elegant stanzas and formal rhythmic diction offer a counter-ballast to her monsters, who are sometimes frightening and at other times poignant. Hers is a world curiously beautiful yet often devoid of hope, a world where the gods invented humans only to lose interest in them. These rich and brilliant poems beg to be read and re-read, their darkness carrying a visceral punch.

—Susan E. Gunter
author of *Dear Munificent Friends:
Henry James's Letters to Four Women*

What strikes one about Patricia Nelson's poems is her often concise and very effective use of language. Many of her lines linger in one's mind, and the visual aspect of her works is thoroughly engaging. The range of subjects, including Greek mythology and Shakespeare, is impressive. I highly recommend this collection for its focused intelligence and poetic vision.

—PETER THABIT JONES
author of *The Fathomless Tides of the Heart:
A Biography of American Poet and
Artist Carolyn Mary Kleefeld*

Centaurs and harpies, both mythological and human monsters, ancient philosophers and intimate narratives—Patricia Nelson populates her world with genre-dismantling characters in this series of exciting, accessible poems that explore both the strengths and frailties of the human condition in all its varied aspects. This potent work is charged with a constant state of in-betweenness, of curiosity, of never-ending continuums, all weaving a sophisticated dialectic that nourished and moved me.

—JOHN SIBLEY WILLIAMS
author of *Skyscrape*
and *The Drowning House*

*With gratitude and fondness for
the mentors of the "Activist" poets:
Lawrence Hart, John Hart,
and Jeanne McGahey.*

Also by Patricia Nelson

Among the Shapes That Fold & Fly, Sugartown Publishing 2013
Spokes of Dream or Bird, Poetic Matrix Press 2017
Out of the Underworld, Poetic Matrix Press 2019
In the Language of Lost Light, Poetic Matrix Press 2021

Contents

Also by Patricia Nelson 6
Acknowledgments 11
MONSTER MONOLOGUES 13
So Many Serpentine Monsters 14
Igor Contemplates His Master 15
The Centaur Chiron 16
A Harpy Warns the Heedless Celebrants 17
Why Monsters Live in Nightmares 18
Minotaur in the Maze 19
Sisyphus Imagines His Final Step 20
Cyclops Senses Humans in His Cave 21
Circe: What My Island Means 23
Monsters with Beautiful Faces 24
Odysseus Grows Tired and Dreams 25
Medea Remembers 26
Medea Revisits the Memory 27
Jason Remembers 28

Jason Revises the Memory 29
Aeetes Speaks of Gods and Heroes 30
Glauce: What Jason's Promise Means to Me 31
Lady MacBeth 32
The Three Weird Sisters Tempt MacBeth 34
MacBeth Lays Blame 35
With New Knowledge, Hamlet Sees His Mother 36
What Iago Wanted 37
Saint Patrick Drives the Snakes Out of Ireland 38
The Wolf in the Story 39

WHAT THE SEERS SAY 41
Medusa Foresees Perseus's Approach 42
Why the Sphinx Is Not Afraid 44
Tiresias Contemplates Light and Dark 45
Tiresias Remembers Childhood 46
Cassandra Unheard 47
The Seer Startled Us 49
Laocoon: *Beware of Greeks Bearing Gifts* 50
Calchas to Agamemnon 51
Proteus Explains Himself 52
A Seer Describes the Gods' Speech 53
A Seer Asks Who Owns the Vision 54
A Sybil Contemplates Dido 55
Why the Sybil Goes on Listening 56
The Dreadful Things She Says 57
Why the Seer Speaks of War and Monsters 58
A Vision Close to Joy 59
A Sybil's Wish 60

TO WHOM IT MATTERS 61
The Gods' Intent 62
The Aftersong 63
The Void 64
Twilight 65

Entering Paradise	66
Metamorphosis	67
First Sailor	68
The Recent Dead	69
The Anteroom	70
The Women of Paradise	71
The Devil Speaks	72
The Briefest of Reprieves	73
They Are Everywhere	74
Diogenes Searched with His Lamp for an Honest Man and Found None	75
Not Stopping at the Edge	76
Orpheus in the Underworld	77
Sleeping Beauty's Steps	78
Pilgrims	79
The Dancers	80
Watcher on a Bluff	81
First House	82
The Fogginess of Time	83
The First Land Animal	84
Title Index	85
First Line Index	89

Acknowledgments

Grateful acknowledgement is made to the following publications in which these poems first appeared, sometimes in different versions:

Amethyst Review: "Metamorphosis"
Anacapa Review: "The Void"
Big Windows: "The Briefest of Reprieves"
Blue Heron Review: "The Women of Paradise" and "Proteus Explains Himself"
Blue Unicorn: "The Wolf in the Story," "Why the Sphinx Is Not Afraid," and "Glauce: What Jason's Promise Means to Me"
Lion and Lilac: "So Many Serpentine Monsters," "Calchas to Agamemnon," and "The Recent Dead"
The Listening Eye: "The Seer Startled Us" and "The Dreadful Things She Says"
Loch Raven Review: "Odysseus Grows Tired and Dreams" and "What Iago Wanted"
Lothlorien Poetry Journal: "The Three Weird Sisters Speak to MacBeth," "MacBeth," "First Sailor," "Igor Contemplates his Master," "The Centaur Chiron," and "A Sibyl's Wish"

MacQueen's Quinterly: "Cyclops Senses Humans in his Cave" and "Why the Seer Speaks of War and Monsters"
Mockingheart Review: "Medea Remembers," "Aeetes Speaks of Gods and Heroes," and "Sisyphus Imagines His Final Step"
Orbis: "Entering Paradise" and "Monsters with Beautiful Faces"
Panoplyzine: "Why Monsters Live in Nightmares" and "First House"
Redwood Writers Poetry Anthology, Beyond Distance: "Medusa Foresees Perseus' Approach," "Circe: What my Island Means," "Diogenes Searched with his Lamp for an Honest Man and Found None," "The Dancers," and "Watcher on a Bluff"
Redwood Writers Anthology, Crossroads: "Cassandra Unheard"
Rockvale Review: "Tiresias Contemplates Light and Dark" and "Medea Revisits the Memory"
Seventh Quarry: "The First Land Animal" and "The Fogginess of Time"
Sheila-Na-Gig: "Why the Sybil Goes on Listening," "Minotaur," "Sleeping Beauty's Steps," and "Orpheus in the Underworld"

MONSTER MONOLOGUES

So Many Serpentine Monsters

This thumb-wide, hissing spine
grew fatter as you slept.

A crooked line now slips
across the daylit stones

and lifts the blue light
in a swaying mouth.

Pause your thudding boots,
your bright-red, stumbling heart.

Let strangeness taste you
with its split, gray tongue.

Igor Contemplates His Master

Do I love my master when I carry
to him what is gray and dead?
My master with his small and twisting lights,
his jars that bubble blue and red in the dark.

My master goes away—when he returns
he bears the bright smell of the air.
And a violence as dense as insects.
Words that thrum and sting.

But I know words that float—butterflies
that ride the light and shade so easily
no one can say if they are white or yellow.
Wings alight in sky and upside-down on water.

My master says the darkness doesn't know
it's dark—dark creatures cannot see the light.
But I see many things: things that have died
and not elided upward. They are so bright to me.

The Centaur Chiron

In Greek mythology, centaurs were unruly half-horse, half-human creatures, except for Chiron, the wisest and kindest. Chiron was skilled in medicine and befriended and tutored many young human heroes.

This one was beautiful and rare. A monster
who forbore enough of what he was
to teach us to be human.

That mission glowed for him
like white stones in a garden.
A path laid upon the wild world.

Good men rode upon his wishes,
his heart that galloped as he
tore away their hesitation

and then led them through the
veering, swerving nearness
of the unforeseen.

When he went too far
and had to die, even the gods
said they were sorry

as they tied him to
the starry, wheeling
tallness of the night.

A Harpy Warns the Heedless Celebrants

In Greek mythology, harpies are half-woman, half-bird creatures, agents of punishment for Zeus. They sometimes appeared at celebratory feasts.

I flap down at the gods' behest
to eye your dance. Raveling beasts
who wheel into visibility
like wet leaves in a gale.

You stomp and feast and sing!
With the wind in your thin and
broken clothes, you tip and bell.
How much you want! And want!

You tug at everything and
ape the revels of the gods.
You're moths about to blacken
on a hot, white lamp!

Oh, the joy that little creatures take
in longings larger than themselves!

Why Monsters Live in Nightmares

Watch the white air fill with birds.
How quickly they cover themselves
in distance and smallness
where you can forget them.

Then the night comes, fills with shapes
you can't hold still with words.
The dream's wet, black oval where
the large, indelible animals glide.

The dragon who enters
wipes her flaming jaw
in the cool mud of her cave.
How bright she is in the dark.

The deformed dog
at the gate to the dead.
How the black air strokes his sides,
his writhing moon-cold hair.

How slyly their shapes elide
across the bottom of the day.
Shadows opening like flowers.

Minotaur in the Maze

> *The minotaur was a mythological bull-headed monster imprisoned in a maze.*

I do not love my prison.
Someone bent the air here.
Angles resound around me
like crickets scraping in the dark.

As I shoulder along the walls
that seem to hold the light,
my yellow eye is like a star
or blowing, turning leaf.

Oh, where is the door that touches
the clear, unstarved sky?

Where are the simple, spacious hungers
in which even monsters ought to live?

Sisyphus Imagines His Final Step

In punishment for tricking the gods, Sisyphus was forced to roll a boulder up a steep hill. The gods told him that if he rolled the stone over the top, they would free him. But each time he neared the top, the boulder would roll back down to the bottom.

One more push will end it.
The pain will fall away and
I'll see ordinary stones below me,
small and bright, as in the falcon's eye.

I'll fill my mouth with the cold sky.
I will be as the gods who shimmered
when they first climbed out of dust.

Each day this belief rises toward
the gods who finger my soul
with height and weight and hope.

Cyclops Senses Humans in His Cave

In Homer's Odyssey, Polyphemus was a one-eyed, sheep-herding, cave-dwelling, man-eating giant, living on the island of Cyclopes. On his voyage home from the Trojan War, Odysseus landed on this island and entered Polyphemus's cave with his men. When the Cyclops sensed their presence, he blocked the entrance to the cave and began eating the men, two at a time. Odysseus got Polyphemus drunk and put out his one eye. Then the men tied themselves to the undersides of Polyphemus's sheep when he let them out to graze in the morning. Polyphemus felt the backs of the sheep to make sure that the men did not escape by riding on them, but doesn't find them where they are cleverly hiding.

i.

At dawn the lambs run, wailing,
from the dark cave to the daylight.
Creatures pale as grief.

I, the jailer, count them,
touching them with memory
and the heat of my hand:

their crooked hair, their gentleness,
the shift of eye and odor,
phrases of sky that leak from their mouths.

I know they see it, the sadness of dawn—
still hold it in their eyes, still call to it.
A call that vibrates like a wish.

Soon I'll shear their purple dawn,
their misery as soft as violets.

ii.

The air in my cave is thicker now. It holds
the muffled shift of cloth and sticks,
the scent of creatures neither good nor gentle.

Their heat and slyness thuds around me.
Their hate whispers in the dark,
a small, blue flame.

How they squeeze the thought of *home*
like a small, gray, weeping gland
or a slow wringing of hands.

They imagine they are free to go there,
growing tall in that wish as if
desire could make them beautiful.

So why are my hands upward?
Why do I stumble toward them,
as if catching rain or light?

Circe: What My Island Means

Odysseus lands on an island where Circe the sorceress lives. She turns his men into pigs.

My island might seem cool and green,
might call to them with sand and river.
My night sky shows them stars
as pale as coiled roses.

And they who sail here might think
that they are beautiful to me.
Beautiful to all who see them.
Beautiful in every sky.

But my island rests upon a shimmer,
a light that searches out the lie.
A breeze in which their faces change
like daylight twisting in a curtain.

Monsters with Beautiful Faces

As a river wrinkles and leaves
in the reeds an undulating moon,

so some monsters lift a face
that stops you like a music.

An impression thin and strange
as candle fire on a current.

And the way she watches you is
stillness with a pulse of light.

Not height or fierceness,
just an absence of velocity.

Odysseus Grows Tired and Dreams

How heavy my memory grows
as I rest awhile and dream
in the forest of light and odor.

Foxes come, and hawks,
and soon those small, mean words
from home that saw me as I was.

The rivers here run clear and bright;
my dreams do not. They seem to say
that I felt joy among the ambiguities,

the afterlight of monsters, the caves
in which the rustling of forms
confused me as to what I love.

So, I lean again on beauty,
a wilderness that pulls me
like the weight below the sea.

Medea Remembers

Medea was a sorceress who aided Jason in his quest for the golden fleece. Medea's father, Aeetes, who owned the golden fleece, assigned Jason many impossible tasks to prevent him from acquiring the fleece. With Medea's help, Jason successfully performed them. Jason married Medea and later abandoned her for another woman. In revenge, Medea killed their children and Jason's new bride.

The horizon where I loved him
was as blue and hot as daylight.

It writhed with yellow birds
and leaf-thin breezes. Everywhere
was curve and sound.

Then as if by magic, absence,
still, cold edges. An emptiness
that altered who I was.

But I will spin a spell:
a wand, a weed,
a wheel full of seeds,

and I'll bend the tale on which
he thought to sail away.
I will blow his blue world out.

Medea Revisits the Memory

On an island where the days bloomed
white and hot, some sickness fed on me:
the heat, the eddy of your nearness.

A god-made love blew through us.
Dark it was, relief like a shovelful of shadows,
a prayer for emptiness.

We came to it by way of winds
of murder and betrayal, weather
that spoke to who we were at heart.

The lightning in me blazed
across the instants when
I might have wondered at it.

Jason Remembers

Storms blew me forward to an
island where the white stones glowed.

Where each day came over the hills
with monsters and a beak of yellow light.

A marvelously wrong place,
made of mind and other dangers.

There I was brave. Each task
they gave me seemed to love me.

A witch appeared, who loved me too,
with magic like fistfuls of pale motes.

Then she loosed the other part of love
where lay a rage as bright as hornets.

Jason Revises the Memory

My memory of it undulates,
a warm green sea, endlessly nudging
the shore with revised animals.

How the meaning evolves, grows
lush and contradictory, a dream
that one can see from many places.

All of us lied, all were lied to.
The villains rose and ebbed,
as victims did, and heroes.

All of us, just curves in the story
on which a little glow or knowledge
seems to fall, for now.

But what of the gods and the heavy dead? Why
have they brought the desert close, this quiet
dust that gleams with monsters?

Aeetes Speaks of Gods and Heroes

> *Aeetes was the father of Medea. He attempted to prevent Jason from obtaining the Golden Fleece by assigning him impossible tasks. Medea defied her father by using magic to help Jason accomplish those tasks.*

Gods don't grieve when heroes fall.
They hear it like a long blue aria,
a deep color they will touch with words.

Each new hero is a wish, a bold thing
they can lift up like a glowing child.
A difference they will want to name.

But things once named, at once
begin to change, to move away
from the moment of the gods' love.

Heroes act according to their wants
and soon betray the gods' love.
The shine in the story dims.

The gods sigh, as if all failures
are audible and final. The hero
turns to look and they are gone.

Glauce: What Jason's Promise Means to Me

Glauce was Jason's new bride, for whom he left Medea. Medea murdered her with a wedding gift of a poisoned robe.

Not certainty or truth—more
a sudden fall in temperature,
as if I've stepped upon a darkness.

I feel the gods within it:
those shadows we give form to
with our foolish wishing.

The gods are air; they talk of
what they want in their god-space
like hawks that paint a sky
with higher hungers.

I seem to hear them soar,
hunting with their eloquence.

Lady MacBeth

> *In Shakespeare's play,* The Tragedy of MacBeth, *three witches tell a victorious Scottish general that he is destined to become king of Scotland. Spurred on by his wife and his own ambition, MacBeth commits a series of murders to seize and hold the throne. His acts cause his reign to unravel.*

i.

My nights are softer than my days,
smoothing every sin with
white: a snow of moonlight.

Fate seems to fold around me—
a shell that recalls the sea
and its small, gray creature.

My dream is almost ripe, a height
I could touch with a whisper—
a hand like a windswept gull.

The time to act is mine,
and oh, so near.
How easy seems the reach.

ii.

For others I see a tide as dark
as mountains, a rise and then a fall.
An eddy of small, drowning men.

Is there a spell to make it still?
Or will it take MacBeth
who cannot walk upon my road:

my wish that wanders like a mist,
my cold, white light
where beasts are hidden.

Oh, he grows old: his knees make
the sound of frost. He shows to me
the simple, white cloth of his face.

How calm I am as I pour him
a mirror of ridicule.

The Three Weird Sisters Tempt MacBeth

Moon strews shadow on the field,
and silver stillness. And we sisters,
casting light that falls unequally
and makes the spaces flower differently.

Light is on us like a skin.
We are mirror, we are bright,
we are the color of winter.
We are always right.

So, show us your unsaid thoughts.
Tell us where you mean to go.
Show us, with your writhing eye,
the hole where you hide your wishes.

The future seems to rustle,
to quicken near you like a breeze.
We'll touch it with thin, sifting
fingers, then we'll go.

MacBeth Lays Blame

The women brought a mirror near me,
pulled me into its floating light. Violence
glowed in the seams of it. A slyness
of witches, part gleam, part murder.

I've met honest enemies as soldiers do,
making simple motions of my hands,
killing quietly, quickly, again and again.
I was made for a warrior's death—

a thing of the body made with rules
and loud, artless words. Not this,
this dark hole that grows deeper.
This fever of omens.

It's the women made this strangeness,
this darkness mixed with bright.

With New Knowledge, Hamlet Sees His Mother

In Shakespeare's play, The Tragedy of Hamlet, Prince of Denmark, *Hamlet learns that his uncle Claudius has seized the throne of Denmark after murdering Hamlet's father and marrying Hamlet's mother.*

I walk slowly in this enigmatic season
where the cold expands and light is halved.
This horizon holding both belief and disbelief.

I now see monsters with a nearer eye.
The mother that I loved begins to speak
and doubt divides me like a shadow.

There is an airless well in me,
in which she falls and falls
and goes out like a star.

I see a barnyard world, filled with
silly creatures moved to murder
by a heat both wild and sincere.

A space where any fool can whirl and cackle.
Where chickens the color of devils run
and some with soft and livid feathers.

What Iago Wanted

In Shakespeare's play, The Tragedy of Othello, *Iago is the villain. He is a trusted subordinate of his general, Othello. Filled with envy and malice toward Othello, he causes Othello's downfall by tricking him into believing his innocent wife is unfaithful and murdering her. He refuses to explain why he has done so.*

The lies I dream are arrows.
They prick the sky and sink.
Where they land shows what I hate:

My well-pleased general singing into
the morning air, his mood full of eels
and cool light like a little lake.

We are told to praise his victories.
To place a story near him
like a mirror filled with silver.

I will bear his golden days,
his summer of lavish yellow dust
and butterflies, his sallow furs.

Then I will take something from him.
The right to pick which lies I tell.

Saint Patrick Drives the Snakes Out of Ireland

Long and quick they are, those skins
that go upon the heat. They glide
on curves they draw in the dust.

How they writhe beside the stones
in a wave of shape and color.
How the light in them pricks my skin.

With the straightness of my stick
I hurl their glowing and sliding
into the cold, green Irish sea.

And now the ache in my arm
is saying one hard throw will do
to make us innocent again.

I call our high and distant God,
to see this gleaming strangeness
I've laid twisting on the water.

The Wolf in the Story

Whoever said that truth is good?
Below the tangled stars
and darkened woods of fairy stories,
it is always clear

that something awful will be there.
He has a hairy light around him
and he shines like a tooth. He is
creeping very near the young and silly.

He tells them freely that he's hungry,
that he's not their guiding angel,
not the curator of mild, gliding stars.
But they never hear him.

They believe that light is meant
to clean their fear away, to smooth
the damp, dark dreams. That whatever
glows in the dark is really good.

They imagine knowledge
loves the children from afar
and remains patient.
That it still loves them as they are.

WHAT THE SEERS SAY

Medusa Foresees Perseus's Approach

Medusa, a beautiful young priestess of Athena, was raped by Poseidon in the temple. Angered at the desecration, Athena turned Medusa into a monster with living snakes for hair and a gaze that turned anyone who looked at her to stone. Perseus eventually beheaded Medea and presented the head to Athena.

I feel him in my dreaming:
the hot white beard of his breath,
the bent shape of his running
repeated in the shadow at his boot.

His shield dims his face
but his wish to end me glows
and shows him as he is:

The coward Perseus who slinks
and sneaks to kill me in my sleep.

His shield lifts an image:
a face that writhes and folds
like snakes in a silver river.
Thinking of it makes his skin go white.

Once my face belonged to me
and spoke the truth of who I was.
I was beautiful and young.
I gleamed and wished no one harm.

Tonight, my dreaming squirms
with hate and longing. I see
my dreadful head begin to fall
and I wish it to be so.

Let him raise it in the dark
like a light, a hook, a fear.

Let the coward look away
as he whispers to it with his sword.

Why the Sphinx Is Not Afraid

If I ever question how I came to be,
the wonder is brief, a yellow gust
like breathing out.

The weight of my soul rests
on my elbows and my lion hocks.
My heart and wings oscillate.

I pose my riddle to the dazzled
creature standing on the dust.
The puzzle I hope he won't solve.

I know one of us must fall into
the dark, the failure to continue
as the animal we were.

But I've lain so long and large
upon the fluttering of days that
death seems small beside me.

A little hush that speaks to others
like the insects going still.

Tiresias Contemplates Light and Dark

In Greek mythology, Tiresias was a blind prophet. He was blinded by an angry god as an adult and given the gift of second sight in compensation. Like many prophets, he often found his warnings disregarded.

I am blind and almost still now.
The dark comes toward me like a weather,
finds me and grows quiet around me.

Here, I speak to the silent, milky dead,
who also wander like an eye
and know the dark with fingers.

The glow cast by the living
sometimes blows toward me
like a fold of music.

Young men go by in shapes of heat,
shadows bending on the rock. They search
for ogres on the dust-bright path.

Their way is steeper than they can
imagine. And it weeps a darkness
even I don't understand.

Tiresias Remembers Childhood

At first I floated in the unseen days,
waxing, turning like a moon.

Then light appeared
and showed me I was small.

Light died each night, but came back stronger,
stranger, like the brightness in the flowers.

And when I slept, I had a child's
nightmares: monsters at my window.

Writhing hands and faces leaning
on the clear as silently as roses.

Then, one day, blackness bathed me
once again in largeness, and I saw it all.

All the men who fought the monsters
that the gods said they had caught.

They filled my sky with silver motes,
a breakage only I could see.

Cassandra Unheard

Cassandra was a Trojan priestess given the gift of prophecy by Apollo but fated to never be believed. Like Laocoon, she tried to warn the Trojans of their impending defeat by the Greeks.

i.

An image rises, walled and still.
My city's towers glow:
wicks already burning.

My sight slides over it
like small clear shapes of rain
showing deaths of many sizes.

My own death—
bright to me.

ii.

The brilliance in a vision ebbs
as stars do, or the folding sea,
the mist that floats away.

In instants I see a roiling city,
the wet dirt where the fallen
will glitter like violets.

But no one listens when I speak.
Not the soldiers, not the crying girls
who will be folded over shoulders.

iii.

Is my voice too high, too crowded?
Is it churning like a sky that tries
to utter all it knows at once:

its wilderness of distance,
the stuttered grief of birdsong,
the loneliness of knowledge.

Why must I go among the unaware—
all those lovely, heedless, unwarned things?

The Seer Startled Us

The seer came and startled us,
a scarlet ibis on a wet, white day.
A warning bright as a wound.

Her commands fell around us
like colors strange to us
among the many that we know.

Is it right that the gods sent a woman
who is odd but not beautiful
to carry light to us?

That she bears in her mouth
their crimson truths?

Laocoon: *Beware of Greeks Bearing Gifts*

They didn't hear Cassandra,
now they walk away from me.
Should seers just stop talking?

All the prophets stilled, who
cannot seem to light today
with the fires of tomorrow?

As the time to act grows small,
those about to die recede, like deer
among the shadow-spotted trees.

And I can only call to them
with ugly truths.

Calchas to Agamemnon

Calchas was a seer in the service of the Greek army. He predicted that the Greeks would not win the Trojan War unless Agamemnon gave his daughter to Apollo as a human sacrifice.

With white and hissing breath
I'll nudge you to the story's end.

I too will touch your murders.
Before they happen, I'll slide over them
a knowing and complicit eye.

This first murder, which the gods demand,
requires both your horror and your honor—
two winds as cold and contradictory
as your unlovely gods.

But something must be excised
from the size of your war
or its correctness

for your victory to be just
as the gods imagined it.

Proteus Explains Himself

*Proteus was a seer who could change his shape. To get
the truth from him, one had to hold him still.*

Remember all those times
the truth strolled past you, stroking
your indifference with its shapes?

Now you must want it, must look up
and find it in its stillness.
The truth has other things to do.

It might be the gull who enters the wind
with a sound of footfalls and goes quiet.
Or the otter in the gleaming river-skin.

Or the leopard's hunger. How her yellow fur
slides through the drying grasses like a river
bearing the many smallnesses of the moon.

As if the truth were not a thing to know
but moonlight moving in the corners
like the whites of eyes.

A Seer Describes the Gods' Speech

There are gods who shriek
and eddy when they think.

Who spit the truth as mist
from hot and hissing rock.

Stones hold the heaviness
of truth, the noise.

The wish within it floats, as though
to know the worst were light.

A Seer Asks Who Owns the Vision

The image is always the same:

a deep slot for the dead
cascading shapes and noise.
It whirls like water and is gone.

Once I thought the visions meant
to pull me toward some consequential act.
That a better outcome lay within me.

But no one listens when I warn.
Perhaps my vision is a mist around me.
Perhaps I whisper the sound of leaves.

Warnings seem to graze us vaguely,
brighten and then dissipate:
an inkling only, like a breath on skin.

Perhaps the vision becomes clearer
as it travels toward the future
where they know they cannot change it

and are far enough away
to find the terror beautiful.

A Sybil Contemplates Dido

*In the Aeneid, Dido was a Carthaginian princess who
fell in love with Aeneas. He abandoned her to pursue
his destiny as the founder of Rome. Grief-stricken, Dido
threw herself into the ocean.*

Her rage shatters like a white wave.
Thoughts so bright and dreadful
they seem to mirror truth.

How large her gestures are,
how they spill upon the pale sand,
as if some star had overfilled the sky.

If she were not so hot and fierce,
if I could touch her like a chilly sea,
would she then be still?

If only words could catch
this moment as it falls,
this shining cup about to break.

Why the Sybil Goes on Listening

Why do I go among these jostlers
every day? This sway of need
as brazen as the yellow lilies.

Is there beauty in so many sorrows
asking to be given weight
and time if they are lucky?

Do I love them? No. I only hear
the smallness of their weeping,
never tall enough to touch the gods.

And I sigh as if I understand
when the gods' justice sometimes
makes a kind of rhyme.

The Dreadful Things She Says

We oracles who breathe
our truths from rocks
that gleam and gabble.

We who call to bell-gray
swaying birds and a yellow sky
that shines so oddly at the rim.

We are sorry when the ones
we warn can't find their way
to the darkened light within our voices.

Even we can dream
that we are different from
the dreadful things we say.

Why the Seer Speaks of War and Monsters

My lamp's circle moves upon
the wider roundness of the beach.

Bright yellow motion on
the hidden yellowness of sand.

At midnight comes a vision
like a shift of silt or shadow.

It's like the noises in my dreams
of late: cries and bangs of war.

The tingle of a monster fingering
the greenest minutes in our leafy places.

It brings a chill that I must utter.
A moon that lights a long, white sea.

A Vision Close to Joy

Do seers only speak to heroes,
those who battle with the gods?

Common, peaceful men are also vessels
for the light. There must be visions right for us.

So please take me without violence
to the things I like to notice.

Wisdom that walks gently toward us
like hooved animals with hanging milk.

A color without weight. A truth
blown near the place of visibility.

A Sybil's Wish

As one leaf casts a shape upon the sky
and many blowing shadows,
I, too, have a shadow-wish
apart from what I say of monsters.

That somewhere there's another door—
a shape of light that anyone might enter,
in which all are disinterred
from hardship and the weather.

Where they can glide as seabirds
glowing by with a wing
in the seams of the wind.

TO WHOM IT MATTERS

The Gods' Intent

The gods invented people,
so they say. Released them
in a shove of clarity and color.

A river of face and bone and want,
feats that glow in their moment and
then float away, bearing the gods'
forgetfulness out to sea.

The gods lean over them awhile,
watch what is beautiful and mortal
as if to lift from darkness
some vague sorrow of their own.

Sometimes they loft one skyward,
then sing its salient virtue in a story
and the dwindling light of their attention.

The Aftersong

Something knowing occupies
the sky. A color or a light
that seems to see.

A kind of wish, imperfect
as the gods and monsters that the mind bleeds.
A direction felt like wind.

Perhaps the weather holds it up.
But should that blowing stop
and drop it where we stand

upon our blue, eroding rock, what
would it disturb with its visions
and then its aftersong

which will never be clear
or long enough?

The Void

Perhaps this shimmer in the
emptiness is nothing—air
doesn't know it owns a shadow.

Doesn't see the leaf-thin light
or the cool, dark tree that bends
like an image on the water's skin.

Doesn't notice its own farness
in which stars blow wonder
open like a flower.

Doesn't love the animals of eye and awe
who reach into the sky with silence
gleaming at their wrists.

Twilight

The solidity of knowledge
is solved rightly
by its intermittence.

The twilight tells it all,
tangles with its views
the light that once you knew.

In the gloaming, a green
grieving bends the colors
like a silent forest.

A love falls into darkness.
It glows like a poppy,
in its brief, red hour.

Entering Paradise

When they enter here, they fold
their hands around the gleam
of worlds they loved.

Let daylight go and grasp
the sad, marveling regret
that transformation brings.

No more greedy mornings
in which their two palms slid
among the colors soft as pelts.

No need for the narrow spine:
knots of green that might assume
the blowing lines of willow.

Just windows breaking,
letting a vast distance in.

Metamorphosis

As swans float through a shadow
bearing the heavy curve of the moon.
As the earth unfolds the flowers'
weightless brilliance.

That is how I thought the Light
would come for me. Would glide
upon me wordlessly, wanting
love, perhaps, or resignation.

And I would assent—to everything,
every list and slant of beauty:

blue wind with yellow birds,
the drifting shore of dawn,
the green speech of a root.

Each small, surprising loss of heaviness.

First Sailor

> *After Dante, "Paradiso": Dante, the voyager, approaches final enlightenment at the apex of Paradise. He is awed and overwhelmed by the knowledge that floods his mind.*

The pilgrim goes wondering
up the floating silver mountain top.
He dreams upon its newness.

A vision of an older wanderer:
the first sailor on the ocean
and the ocean god who slept beneath the voyage.

The sailor spoke the prayer of daring:
the squeak of wheel and wood,
the sigh of a crooked wind.

The sky was loud with oars and flying cloths.
The ship dragged its shadow shape above
the sea god's leaf-quick, sleeping eyes.

The shadow widened, staining,
like a dye, the sea god's dreams.
He rose and shook the sky with anger.

Dangling on his thumb: a storm,
the air between the waves,
the sailor on his bit of wood.

Then he stopped and softened like a gale,
filling the sailor's sky with gleaming rain
and the unexplainable gift of mercy.

The Recent Dead

I stand among the recent dead.
We lift our hands, hold out
our souls like small gray stones.
I sense a fall, a cost.

Is this the place where
we are told that we are lost?
That the world grows
wider by our absence?

What rises from our palms
like prayer or a scent of roses?
One sadness, brief
among the longer truths.

The Anteroom

Who will let these wishers in?

They push upon the thinnest slots
like rodents or the mail.

They cite the right gods
and a wish to enter.

A wish in need of a wind.

The Women of Paradise

The real women they remember
now seem heavy, full of earth—
white roses black with bees.

They want tall, transparent creatures
hanging brightness near them
like a silver sleeve.

Women to gather the darting light,
to feel the many wishes
swimming in their skin.

Whose job it is to promise. To lift
the light and play it like a horn
for the eager and imperfect.

The Devil Speaks

They come here without color.
Shadows from the flowering world.

They recall looking upward. Air
that dropped light and water on them.

All the things they knew or wished.
The thoughts that made them who they were.

Perhaps, for them,
a tale better left unfolded.

No one will hear their wishing now,
or care, and only I am near.

The Briefest of Reprieves

We are free now. Taller, wiser
than the myths of childhood.
Gone, the sins we held like stones.

We touch our chests with the shape
of the crossroads. We begin to forget
the singe of shadow on our foreheads.

Look around. No higher beings here.
No devil to touch us like a whirlwind.
No angels turning in the sky like bells.

But freedom leaves a hole. Do we miss
the pleasure of an undertow, the hiss
of demon in the foaming wave?

Do we want a cave where we run deeper in,
twisting like the shadows on the walls?
In dreams, we all call out to fear and wonder.

They Are Everywhere

Where are the forgotten gods,
old in their glimmering,
quiet in their cold sleep?

Call them with your stories,
your rivers filled with light.

Imagine that you see
them move, like moons
or fish among the deepest rocks.

Imagine they are everywhere
like floating thoughts.

Diogenes Searched with His Lamp for an Honest Man and Found None

They marvel at my lamp,
the light like a flutter of leaf
that shows them as they are.

No one in a fever holds the truth
against his forehead like a pleasant thing,
a moment cool as glass.

No one who is grieving
presses it against her heart.
No one glows when it enters them.

No one guesses what it needs:
That thing to be loved long and utterly,
loved without art or darkness.

Not Stopping at the Edge

Some edges you will come to
and forget to stop.

Tall and creatured forests
in which all the colors fall

and your weight abuts a steepness
that will reach for you one day.

You'll go deeper, past the floes of
light, the cold and leafy birds.

Watch your shadow holding
each white pebble.

Orpheus in the Underworld

In Greek mythology, Orpheus was a legendary musician who charmed everyone with his singing and lyre-playing. When his bride Eurydice died, he went to the underworld and charmed Hades into letting him bring her back to the world of the living. Hades set one condition, that Orpheus could not look back at her while leading her out of the underworld. Orpheus could not stop himself from looking, and when he turned around, she disappeared back into the underworld.

There is a round door into loss,
where love may circle slowly
like a bear and enter.

The air in the underworld
is soft and gray. It flutters
like the dust in which
the ravens wash their wings.

I must bring her back to light
without holding her colors with my eyes
or touching the thought
of her dissolution and decay.

But there are bloodless creatures here
walking without heat or odor.
Their rustling confuses me.

I must winnow her sound
from the music of their darkness
and the loudness of my hope.

Sleeping Beauty's Steps

How clear her footprints
were upon the dust.
Both shape and absence.

And how he wished
to gather them, to know
what her path said to her.

As if her walking were a dream
that anyone might pass through
without harm

and the creatures stirring near
the path were only metaphor
for his own love and yearning.

As if any difficulty in it
moved in time with beauty.

Pilgrims

So many crossed the dunes
like seasons or recurring night.

As if just walking on would
bring them light or grace.

Creatures of small variations
who bend and die like grasses.

One can't see wishes in the traces,
how tall, how fierce the walking was.

Their losses lie below the moon
like white dust on an altar.

The Dancers

After Joy Harjo, "Exile of Memory"

In just the right dark,
just the right distance,
the dancers return,

ride around and through us
on blossoms of dust,
a rattle of black hooves.

The dancers touch us
like weights or elements,
a shifting as of pebbles.

Come swim in the slow dissolution
of mountains, they say, the tide of sky.
Come wear the eagle's yellow, floating eye.

Watcher on a Bluff

The skater is a water flower.
Weightless, moved by moon
and tide and solitude.

Thin as memory or
the color of a star. A clear
bowl glowing in a hand.

Far away, a day that I recall
as char or bullet. Anger spinning
without grace or floating.

She's a farther, lighter thing
alive on a still and silver edge.

First House

Sometimes she loves innocence,
her first house of words. The window
in which blue light scuds forever.

The garden of small, tended trees
that shed a pleasant noise and scent
and day-bright shadows on the wall.

Sometimes she remembers tended light
as truer light. How it soothed her,
how she loved it in return.

All the light seems unkempt now.
Unmendable. Unsayable.

The Fogginess of Time

After Joy Harjo

Move the dark points of your eyes,
your iris full of damp and light.

See the moon in the wide night
turning her battered stones
and the falling colors of rain,

dark bees riding a transparent
breeze, gathering the glassy gusts,
the unsayable colors.

Find the clouds of time in each. Touch it
with the stillness in your fingers.

The First Land Animal

On the plainness of the land
the first animal.

The vessel walking on
the drifting color of the sand.

It touches gray,
it touches brown.

Then the swaying air,
in which it alters.

Its journey visible
in all its thirst.

Title Index

Aeetes Speaks of Gods and Heroes 30
A Harpy Warns the Heedless Celebrants 17
A Seer Asks Who Owns the Vision 54
A Seer Describes the Gods' Speech 53
A Sybil Contemplates Dido 55
A Sybil's Wish 60
A Vision Close to Joy 59
Calchas to Agamemnon 51
Cassandra Unheard 47
Circe: What My Island Means 23
Cyclops Senses Humans in His Cave 21
Diogenes Searched with His Lamp for an Honest Man
   and Found None 75
Entering Paradise 66
First House 82
First Sailor 68
Glauce: What Jason's Promise Means to Me 31
Igor Contemplates His Master 15

Jason Remembers 28
Jason Revises the Memory 29
Lady MacBeth 32
Laocoon: *Beware of Greeks Bearing Gifts* 50
MacBeth Lays Blame 35
Medea Remembers 26
Medea Revisits the Memory 27
Medusa Foresees Perseus's Approach 42
Metamorphosis 67
Minotaur in the Maze 19
Monsters with Beautiful Faces 24
Not Stopping at the Edge 76
Odysseus Grows Tired and Dreams 25
Orpheus in the Underworld 77
Pilgrims 79
Proteus Explains Himself 52
Saint Patrick Drives the Snakes Out of Ireland 38
Sisyphus Imagines His Final Step 20
Sleeping Beauty's Steps 78
So Many Serpentine Monsters 14
The Aftersong 63
The Anteroom 70
The Briefest of Reprieves 73
The Centaur Chiron 16
The Dancers 80
The Devil Speaks 72
The Dreadful Things She Says 57
The First Land Animal 84
The Fogginess of Time 83
The Gods' Intent 62
The Recent Dead 69
The Seer Startled Us 49
The Three Weird Sisters Tempt MacBeth 34
The Void 64

The Wolf in the Story 39
The Women of Paradise 71
They Are Everywhere 74
Tiresias Contemplates Light and Dark 45
Tiresias Remembers Childhood 46
Twilight 65
Watcher on a Bluff 81
What Iago Wanted 37
Why Monsters Live in Nightmares 18
Why the Seer Speaks of War and Monsters 58
Why the Sphinx Is Not Afraid 44
Why the Sybil Goes on Listening 56
With New Knowledge, Hamlet Sees His Mother 36

First Line Index

A
An image rises, walled and still 47
As a river wrinkles and leaves 24
As one leaf casts a shape upon the sky 60
As swans float through a shadow 67
At dawn the lambs run, wailing 21
At first I floated in the unseen days 46

D
Do I love my master when I carry 15
Do seers only speak to heroes 59

G
Gods don't grieve when heroes fall 30

H
Her rage shatters like a white wave 55
How clear her footprints 78
How heavy my memory grows 25

I

I am blind and almost still now 45
I do not love my prison 19
I feel him in my dreaming 42
If I ever question how I came to be 44
I flap down at the gods' behest 17
In just the right dark 80
I stand among the recent dead 69
I walk slowly in this enigmatic season 36

L

Long and quick they are, those skins 38

M

Moon strews shadow on the field 34
Move the dark points of your eyes 83
My island might seem cool and green 23
My lamp's circle moves upon 58
My memory of it undulates 29
My nights are softer than my days 32

N

Not certainty or truth—more 31

O

On an island where the days bloomed 27
One more push will end it 20
On the plainness of the land 84

P

Perhaps this shimmer in the 64

R

Remember all those times 52

S

So many crossed the dunes 79
Some edges you will come to 76
Something knowing occupies 63

Sometimes she loves innocence 82
Storms blew me forward to an 28

T

The gods invented people 62
The horizon where I loved him 26
The image is always the same 54
The lies I dream are arrows 37
The pilgrim goes wondering 68
The real women they remember 71
There are gods who shriek 53
There is a round door into loss 77
The seer came and startled us 49
The skater is a water flower 81
The solidity of knowledge 65
The women brought a mirror near me 35
They come here without color 72
They didn't hear Cassandra 50
They marvel at my lamp 75
This one was beautiful and rare. A monster 16
This thumb-wide, hissing spine 14

W

Watch the white air fill with birds 18
We are free now. Taller, wiser 73
We oracles who breathe 57
When they enter here, they fold 66
Where are the forgotten gods 74
Whoever said that truth is good? 39
Who will let these wishers in? 70
Why do I go among these jostlers 56
With white and hissing breath 51

www.ingramcontent.com/pod-product-compliance
Lightning Source LLC
Chambersburg PA
CBHW010046090426
42735CB00020B/3409